MAP of YOU

By Sophie Williams

This map belongs to: _____

THE START!

Welcome to the start of a very special journey; a journey into the magical landscape of YOU! In this book, you will visit your mountains of strength and your wetlands of weakness. You will chart your forest of fears and weather the storms of your anger. You'll learn and question and explore all the things that make you, you!

The road to inner peace and contentment is long and winding, but as the Chinese philosopher, Lao Tzu, once said, 'The journey of a thousand miles begins with a single step'. So lace up your boots and pack your bag... it's time to set off!

Start by filling in some personal details:

Name:_____ Date of birth:_____

Where I was born:_____ Where I live:_____

Eye colour:_____ Hair colour:_____ Height:_____

Today I feel:_____

I love myself because:_____

_____

SELF PORTRAIT SUNFLOWERS

Draw your face in this flower!

Draw yourself in your favourite outfit in this flower!

Describe yourself in one sentence:

Describe yourself in three words:

DESIGNING YOUR WORLD...

You are in control of the Map of You! You can make your world as wacky and as beautiful as you want it to be!

Where is the BEST place in your world to visit? Draw it here:

What is your world called?

_____

Circle the words that best describe your world:

Hot   Calm   Busy   Wild   Bright   Natural

Big   Snowy   Small   Magical   Modern

Exciting   Woodland   Ocean   Mountains   Desert

Beach   Grand   Cities   Countryside   Rivers

Quiet   Loud   Tranquil   Bustling   Fantasy

Real   Paradise   Tropical   Advanced

Spooky   Beautiful   Dramatic   Relaxing   Fun

What are the laws of your land? Write three of them below:

L A W S

1._____
_____
_____

2._____
_____
_____

3._____
_____
_____

Every place needs a good motto! Some examples are 'The city that never sleeps' and 'Where everybody can be a somebody!' What would the motto of your world be?

_____

_____

Draw a view looking out at your world from indoors:

Design a flag for your world. You can use the shapes and symbols underneath for inspiration.

Where would you live in your world? In a house? A cave? A castle?! Draw it below:

The sun represents unity.

The moon symbolises divinity or godliness.

Stars represent energy.

A square symbolises balance and equality.

The triangle represents strength and power.

The rainbow represents peace and prosperity.

SURVIVAL KIT

As you navigate your way around the landscape of YOU, you'll need to be prepared for some tough environments. Pack an 'emotional survival kit' to help you out in times of trouble.

A grounding object like a polished pebble that reminds you of a good place. Moving the pebble around in the palm of your hand can be calming and distract you from dark thoughts. Draw it here:

A sachet of your favourite tea or other warm drink. Draw it here:

A list of things to be grateful for, so you can remind yourself of the good things in life.

A list of things that you thought that you'd never get over, but did.

A comfort item from someone you love
(scarf/ t-shirt/ jumper). Draw it here:

A playlist of songs that make you happy.

A mantra that you can repeat to
calm yourself down. Write it here:

A 'read this in case of emergency' letter
reminding yourself to stay positive.

A copy of your favourite
book. Write the title here:

Your favourite chocolate bar.
Draw it here:

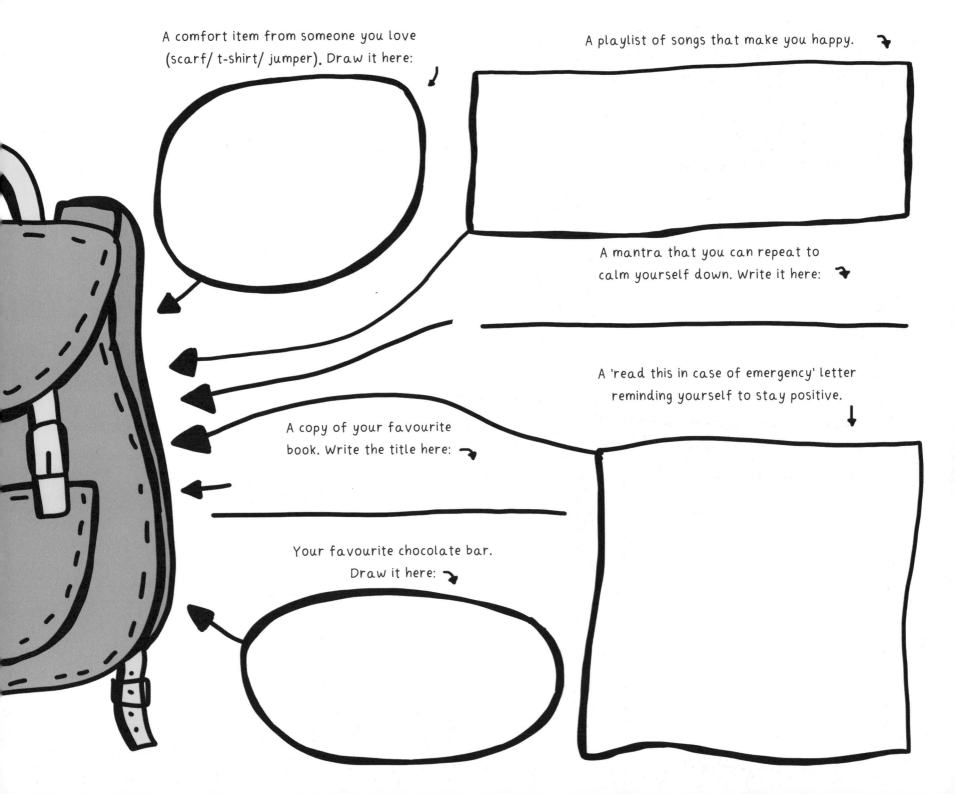

WHICH PERSONALITY TYPE SUITS YOU?

Are you a peacemaker, adventurer, investigator or protector? Answer the questions below and find out which best represents you!

1. What do you value most in a friend?

A. Kindness ☐

B. Fun ☐

C. Reliability ☐

D. Ambition ☐

2. Which of these are you best at?

A. Working in a team ☐

B. Taking risks ☐

C. Organising things ☐

D. Standing up for yourself ☐

3. How would you rather spend the day?

A. Hanging out with friends ☐

B. Exploring a new place ☐

C. Making something ☐

D. Learning a new skill ☐

4. What job would you prefer?

A. Artist ☐

B. Travelling circus performer ☐

C. Scientist ☐

D. Teacher ☐

5. What do you find the hardest?

A. Standing up for yourself ☐

B. Sticking to a routine ☐

C. Doing something you don't want to ☐

D. Not sticking to a plan ☐

6. Which best describes you?

A. Sensitive and empathetic ☐

B. Fun loving and all over the place! ☐

C. Strong and independent ☐

D. Hard-working and driven ☐

7. Which bird do you relate to the most?

A. Peaceful dove ☐

B. Colourful parrot ☐

C. Strong eagle ☐

D. Wise owl ☐

8. You've fallen out with a friend. How do you react?

A. Apologise immediately! ☐

B. Forget about it and have fun! ☐

C. Stand your ground ☐

D. Write them a message explaining how you feel ☐

9. Your family surprises you with a holiday you knew nothing about! How do you react?

A. Nervous but excited ☐

B. SO excited! ☐

C. Let me research some daily activities! ☐

D. WORST nightmare... I like to be in charge! ☐

10. Which colour best represents you?

A. White ☐

B. Yellow ☐

C. Green ☐

D. Red ☐

RESULTS!

Look back through your answers. Which letter did you tick most often? If you got....

Mostly 'A's......

You are a Peacemaker!

Mostly 'B's......

You are an Adventurer!

Mostly 'C's......

You are an Investigator!

Mostly 'D's......

You are a Protector!

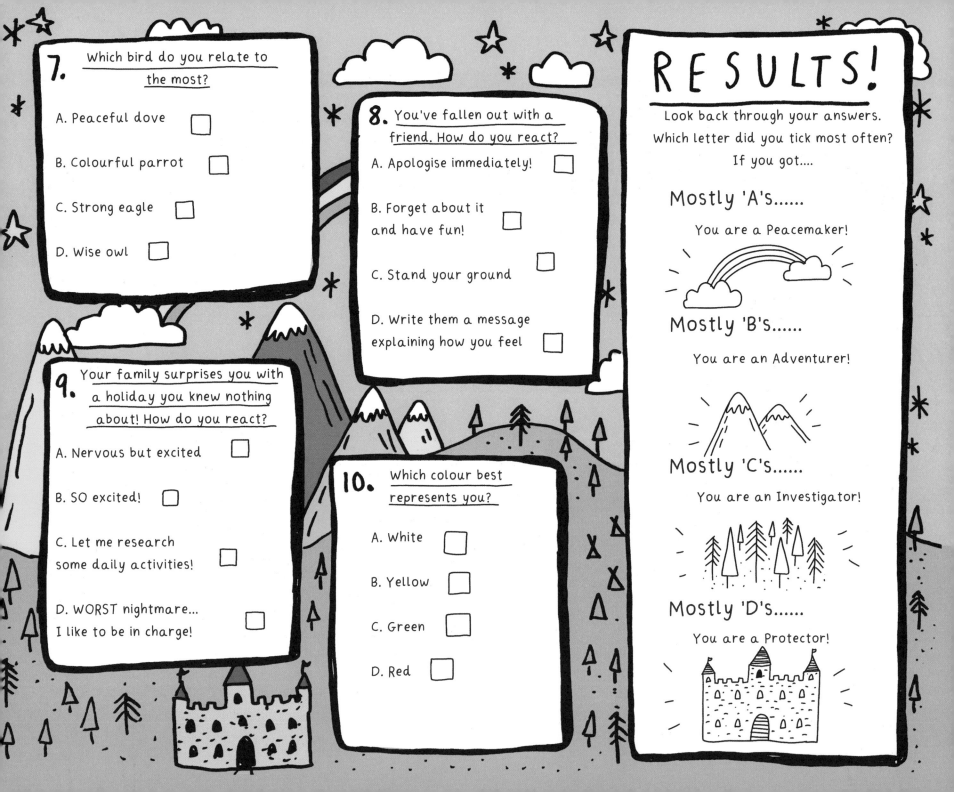

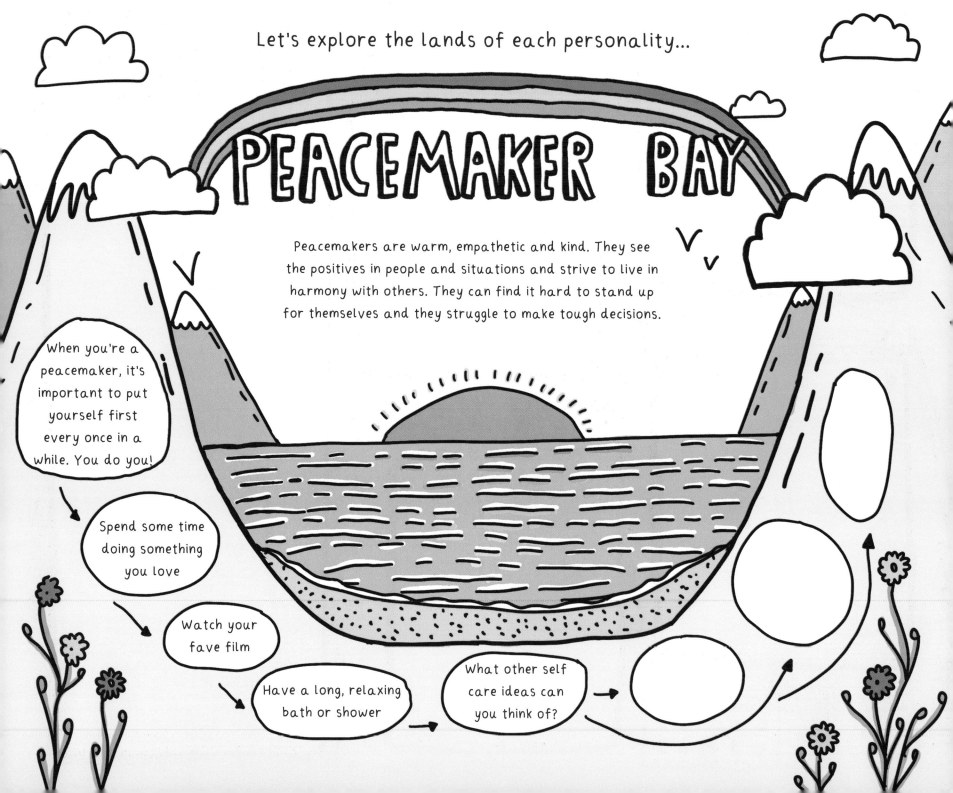

ADVENTURER'S CAMP

Adventurers are fun loving, spontaneous and always up for exploring new places and meeting new people. Nothing fazes them, which is why they don't believe in planning! They can get bored easily, which means they sometimes leave things unfinished.

If you could go anywhere in the world, where would you go?

What activity have you always longed to try?

Draw a memento from a great adventure you've had

Obviously, adventurers LOVE an adventure!
Record an adventure you've had below:

Date:_____ Location:_____ Name of adventure:_____

Description :_____

_____

_____

What I learned :_____

_____

INVESTIGATOR'S WOODS

Investigators are strong, independent, practical, creative, honest and rational.
They are great at thinking things through and are confident in their opinions.
Sometimes they can be stubborn and can struggle in certain social situations.
Investigators find it very satisfying to make things.

What is your favourite thing you've ever made? Draw or write it here!

What is something you would like to get better at making?

If you could make ANYTHING what would it be? Draw it here:

PROTECTOR'S CASTLE

Protectors are strong, loyal, reliable and sure of themselves. They are excellent at planning, which makes them great leaders — they can really get things done! Protectors can sometimes be a bit controlling and get frustrated with people who don't do things their way.

Imagine you're directing a movie... you're in control!

Draw the movie poster!

What would it be called?

_____

What type of movie is it?

_____

Who would you cast?

_____

_____

Write a short outline of the story:

_____

_____

_____

_____

_____

YOUR ROCKS

We all need rocks in our lives — people who accept us for who we are and who stand by us through thick and thin. They could be parents, siblings, friends... Who are your rocks? You might have one rock or several. Sometimes we have big rocks and smaller rocks that we rely on in different ways.

Draw or write the names of the people who you know will always be by your side.

Write the ways in which your rocks support you in the shapes below.

Never take the rocks in your life for granted!

What do you do for your rocks? Are there ways in which you help them too?

Sometimes, looking at the bigger picture allows us to have some perspective on who we are and what drives us.

HAZY

What is in your heart? What do you truly love?

Where do you see yourself in five years' time?

What is your driving force? What fuels you?

How do you see your passion shaping your future?

Where do you see yourself in ten or even twenty years' time?

HORIZONS

What do your future horizons look like? How will you get there? Dream big!

MOUNTAINS of __STRENGTH__

Let's celebrate the BEST things about you!

What do you think people admire in you?

Name five of your strengths:

What are your best features?

Write a love letter to yourself:

Dear _____
_____
_____
_____
_____
_____
_____
_____
_____
_____
_____
_____
_____
_____
_____
_____
_____
_____
_____
_____
_____
_____

WETLANDS of WEAKNESS

To be flawed is to be human. Embrace your flaws along with your strengths!

What things could you do to be your best self?

What do you consider your weaknesses?

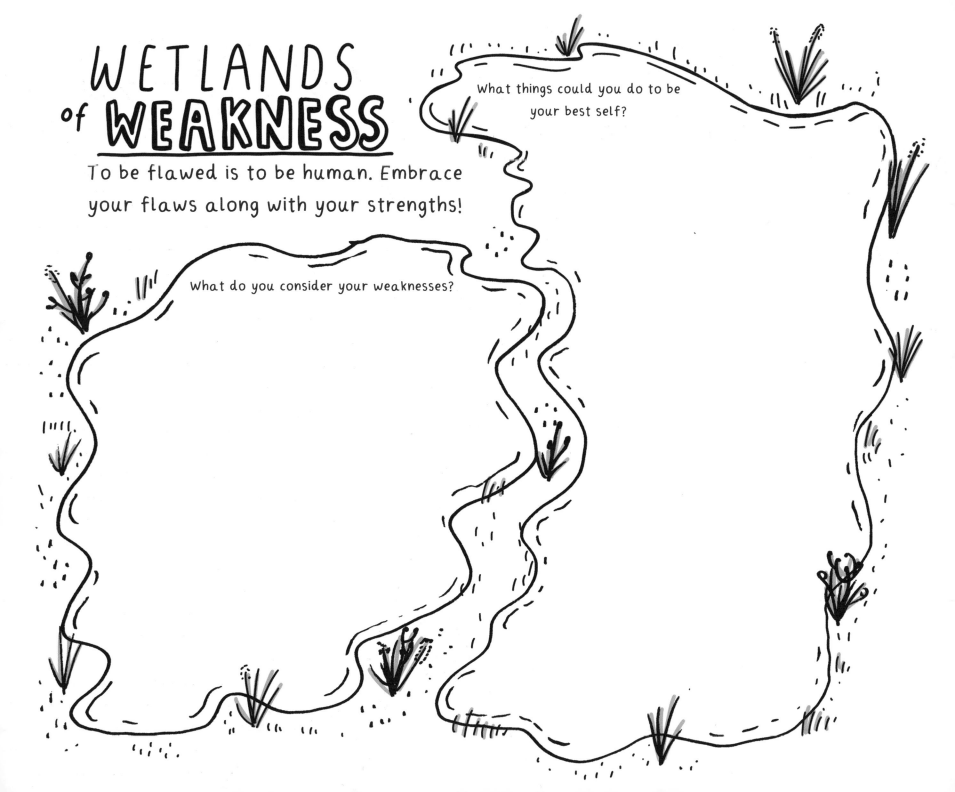

If someone you love had the same weaknesses as you,
what would you say to them?

When we learn to accept our weaknesses rather than
fight them, we find the strength to be better people.

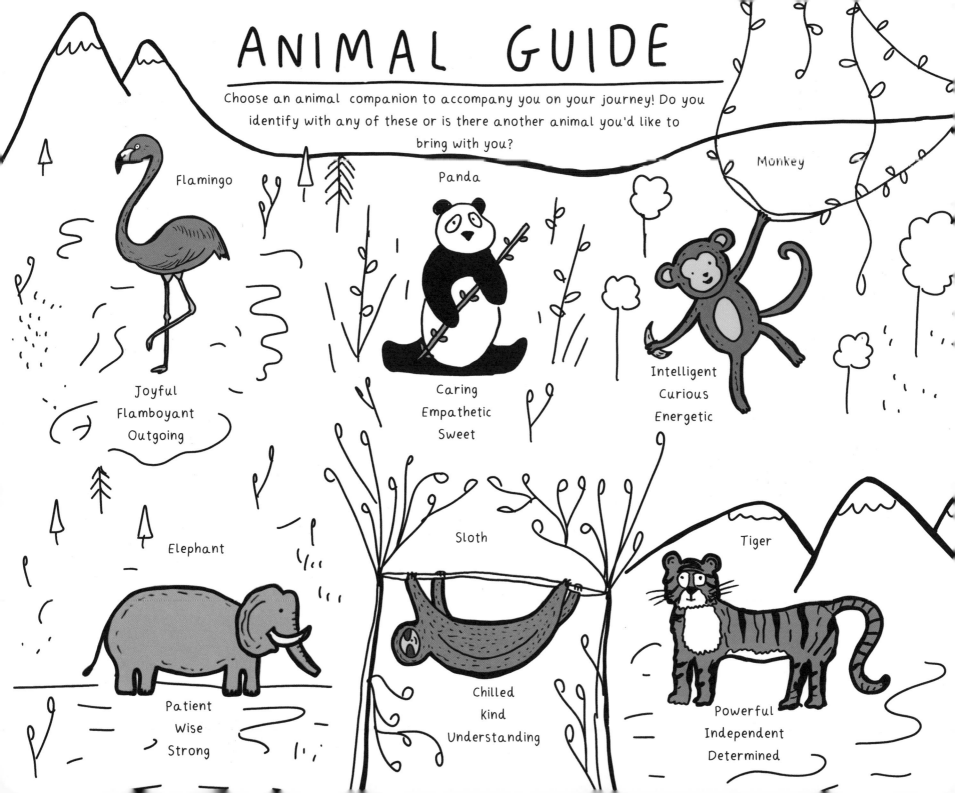

CERTIFICATE of ADOPTION

OFFICIAL ADOPTION

Animal name: _____

Animal species: _____

I am adopting this animal because:

_____

_____

Animal's favourite food: _____

Animal's favourite activity: _____

Carer's name (that's you):

_____

Carer's signature:

_____

congratulations!

Draw your animal here:

CONFIDENCE COCOON

Imagine you're a caterpillar, safe in your cocoon,
growing into your future self.

What are the things that nourish you and help you grow?

_____
_____
_____
_____
_____
_____
_____
_____
_____
_____
_____
_____
_____

Decorate the cocoon with patterns
and symbols of strength. ♡

Decorate your butterfly with confidence!

To fulfil our potential, we eventually need to break out of our cocoon. What are the things that hold you back from breaking free?

_____
_____
_____
_____
_____
_____
_____
_____
_____

Have there been moments in your life when you have felt like the butterfly you were always meant to be? What were they?

STORMY SKIES

Anger can be destructive and can hurt people around us. But it is also an important survival tool, protecting us from emotional or physical harm.

Everybody expresses anger in a different way. Some people become aggressive, whilst others take their anger out on themselves. How does your anger look? Draw your storm clouds here!

How does your anger express itself? _____
_____
_____
_____
_____

What are some things that you've said or done in anger? _____
_____
_____
_____
_____

How have people responded?
_____
_____
_____
_____

Does your anger pass quickly or does it linger?
_____
_____
_____
_____

To control our anger we first have to recognise it.

Anger causes a rush of adrenaline, so these are some common symptoms:

Your breathing quickens

Your fists or jaws clench

Your heart beats faster

Your body becomes tense

Anger is most destructive when it explodes out of us. Try to give yourself time to think before you react.

Count to ten.

Take yourself away from the situation.

Talk to a person you trust who is not connected to the situation.

Try calming breathing exercises.

Don't focus on things you cannot change. Instead use your energy to find positive solutions that will help you feel better.

Anger can also energise us to make changes and solve problems. Are there issues that enrage you? Maybe it's a big issue like the environment, or maybe it's something closer to home. If we channel the passion of our anger properly, we can affect positive change.

What's a cause that gets you riled up?

_____

_____

_____

Design a protest placard!

MESSAGE
IN A
BOTTLE

It's important to communicate with the people in your life, so they can respond to your thoughts and feelings.

If you were stranded on a desert island and you could send a message in a bottle to anyone in your life, who would it be?

_____

What would it say? Write it here!

It's also important to communicate with yourself.

Creativity lets out feelings and ideas that sometimes we didn't even know we had.

Use this page to doodle or write spontaneously. Don't think too hard about what you're drawing or writing — just let it flow.

If we know how we are feeling,
we can express it to others.

What are some things that make it hard for you to communicate?

_____

_____

_____

_____

_____

_____

What could you do to make it easier?

_____

_____

_____

_____

_____

_____

FOREST of FEARS

Fear is a natural response that evolved to help us avoid danger. Everyone experiences irrational fears - the dark, dogs, enclosed spaces... Do you have any irrational fears? Write them inside the Forest of Fears.

Usually we learn to cope with our fears, but sometimes they grow into phobias that can take control of our lives. Do you have any phobias that stop you from doing things? Draw them as the monster that haunts the forest.

escape the forest with the...
FEAR LADDER

Exposing ourselves to the source of our fear in small, controlled ways can help us overcome it. Someone who is afraid of dogs might spend time looking at dogs from behind a window. Then they might spend time with a friendly puppy and gradually move onto petting larger dogs. This is called desensitisation.

Pick a situation that you avoid because it makes you feel anxious. Write it at the top of the ladder next to number five.

Think of four steps that you could take to build up to confronting that situation. Rate the anxiety level of each step out of ten.

Once you decide to work on your ladder, you can move up from the bottom or randomly pick a step and practice it over and over.

Celebrate yourself each time you take a step onto your ladder!

	Anxious Situation	Anxiety Rating
5		/10
4		/10
3		/10
2		/10
1		/10

Worry gives a small thing a big shadow.

Draw your tiny worry here

Then draw the shadow it casts when you're
not feeling strong enough to cope.

the MEADOW of MINDFULNESS

Mindfulness is a mental state that is achieved by focusing your awareness on the present moment, while calmly accepting your feelings, thoughts and bodily sensations.

Here are some simple ways you can be mindful:

Breathing:

Tune into your breathing. If you focus your mind on controlling your breath, you can free it from the things that are distracting you from being in the moment.

Concentrate on inhaling for three counts and exhaling for three counts.

Pretend you're blowing bubbles: take a deep, slow breath in and then breathe out slowly and steadily, filling the bubble without popping it.

Draw with your breath. Use the space below to draw lines guided by the pace of your breathing. Shut your eyes and let the pen wander where it will.

Grounding:

This is a simple technique to help you focus your mind and be present. Pay attention to the things going on around you and how your body is responding to them.

Write down five things you can see:

Write down four things you can touch:

Write down three things you can hear:

Write down two things you can smell:

Write down one thing you can taste:

Do this whenever you feel overwhelmed. You don't have to write the answers down every time, just bring your attention back to the present by noting the ways in which your senses are responding to your environment.

Yoga is a spiritual discipline that combines breathing exercises with body movements, helping you feel present and calm. It's also fun to create shapes with your body. Here are some simple poses you can try!

Tree Pose:
. Place the sole of your foot on your inner calf or thigh.
. Ground yourself through the opposite leg and foot.
. Place your hands together above your head or at your heart.
. Concentrate on your balance. How long can you stand without wobbling?

Butterfly Pose:
. Sit on your buttocks with your spine tall.
. Bend your legs and put the soles of your feet together.
. Flutter your wings like a butterfly to help with flexibility!

Triangle Pose:
. Stand in a star position; legs and arms out wide.
. Turn one foot to the side keeping your arms straight. Bend through your hips over the foot that's pointing out.
. Rest your hand on your shin or ankle and reach your other arm up to the sky.
. Feel the stretch in your side and breathe into it.

Child's Pose:
. Spread your knees wide.
. Let your belly rest on your thighs.
. Put your forehead down.
. Reach your arms out in front of you or place them by your sides.
. Feel your spine stretching as you let all your tension go.

Comfort ZONE

A comfort zone is a place where everything feels safe and familiar. Anxiety and stress levels are low in your comfort zone. You're in control, so you can relax!

Draw a cosy shelter that is safe from all the scary things outside. Decorate it and make it lovely!

What objects remind you of people and places you love? Draw them here – they will be an important part of your safe space.

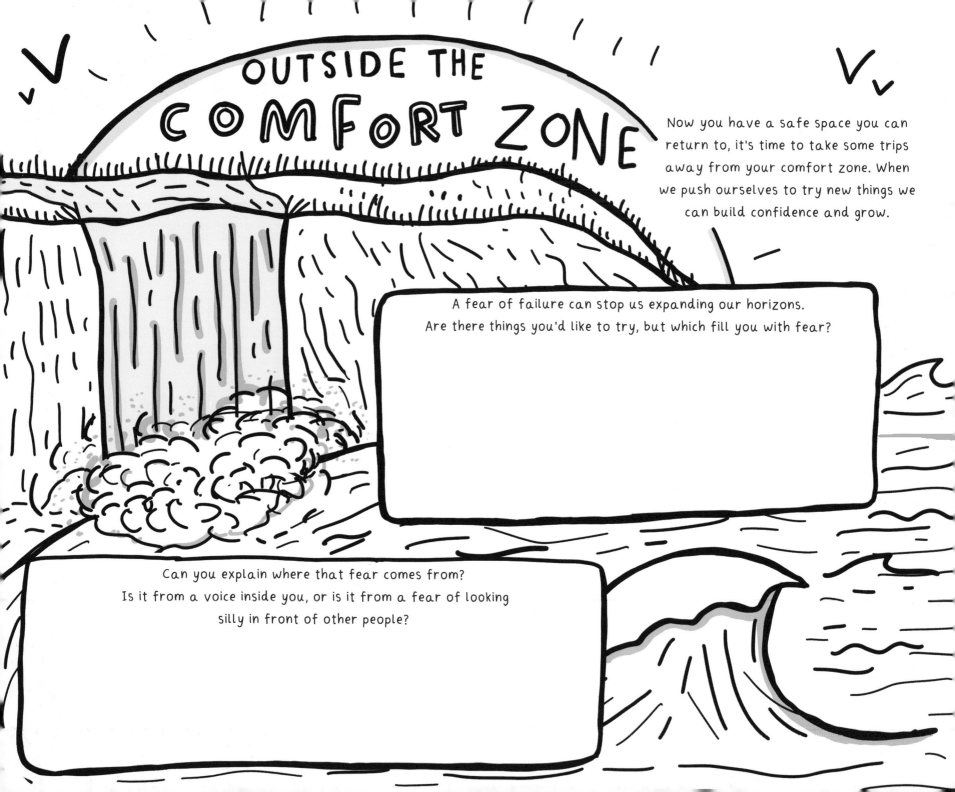

OUTSIDE THE COMFORT ZONE

Now you have a safe space you can return to, it's time to take some trips away from your comfort zone. When we push ourselves to try new things we can build confidence and grow.

A fear of failure can stop us expanding our horizons.
Are there things you'd like to try, but which fill you with fear?

Can you explain where that fear comes from?
Is it from a voice inside you, or is it from a fear of looking silly in front of other people?

Imagine you're doing the thing that scares you. Visualise the best-case scenario and the worst-case scenario:

BEST:

WORST:

Devise a backup plan if things go wrong:

Try to silence the negative voices in your head. A positive outlook will give you the confidence to break free. Say out loud 'I can do this'. Now shout it. 'I CAN DO THIS!'

Only those who dare to fail greatly can ever achieve greatly.
– Robert Kennedy

INTROVERT or EXTROVERT?

Do you feel the need to always be centre stage, or are you more comfortable watching from the sidelines?
Take this quiz to find where you are on the introversion spectrum.

1. You're busy with an important piece of schoolwork when a friend starts telling you about his problems in great detail. You:

A. Don't dare interrupt.
B. Give him some time, your work can wait for a bit.
C. Listen with half an ear but keep doing your work.
D. Interrupt and explain that you are really busy at the moment.

2. You've been waiting for a doctor's appointment for almost an hour. You:

A. Amuse yourself quietly with a book or a magazine.
B. Look at the clock on the wall impatiently, but say nothing.
C. Ask your mum loudly why the doctor is always running late.
D. Go to the reception desk and ask how much longer it will be. You don't have all day!

3. Your teacher is introducing a new subject you know a lot about. You:

A. Keep your knowledge to yourself.
B. Listen to the teacher and raise your hand when it's time to answer questions.
C. Offer your insights as soon as an opportunity arises.
D. Interrupt so everyone can benefit from your expertise.

4. It's your birthday! Your ideal party is:

A. Going for a nice meal with your family.
B. One or two friends come over for pizza and a movie.
C. A fun outdoor activity with four or five friends.
D. An epic party – everyone's invited!

5. You're in charge of a group project and someone disagrees with your approach. You:

A. Let them take charge – they'll probably do a better job of it.
B. Agree with some of their ideas and adjust your approach.
C. Defend your own point of view.
D. Interrupt them and put them in their place.

6. You crack a joke but nobody seems to notice. You:

A. Think it's for the best - it wasn't that funny anyway.
B. Wait to share it with your best friend later.
C. Try again after a few minutes have passed.
D. Keep telling it until they pay attention.

7. You have a free day and none of your friends are around. You:

A. Heave a sigh of relief and stay at home all day in your PJs.
B. Take it easy, watch some telly and maybe go for a little walk.
C. Feel a bit bored, but stay productive and catch up on creative projects and homework.
D. Stomp about loudly, moaning about what a boring day you're having.

8. Your friends are talking about a TV show you haven't seen. You:

A. Stay silent and don't mention you haven't seen it.
B. Ask questions to find out more about it.
C. Pretend you've watched it and loved it.
D. Change the subject.

9. You say something that is misinterpreted. You:

A. Agonise and feel terrible but say nothing.
B. Apologise profusely, even though you didn't mean anything by it.
C. Explain what you meant and clear the issue up.
D. Tell the person they got it all wrong.

10. A new person has joined your class. You:

A. Avoid eye contact.
B. Smile from across the room but say nothing.
C. Say 'hi' and wait to see if they start a conversation.
D. Introduce yourself and your friends... if they look cool enough!

11. A friend arrives late for a date. You:

A. Don't mention it.
B. Sulk but don't say anything.
C. Tell them they're late but then move on.
D. Make a scene and tell them off publicly.

12. You've lost an important piece of schoolwork. You:

A. Stay up all night stressing but don't say anything.
B. Search madly, hoping someone will offer to help.
C. Get everyone to help look for it.
D. Accuse the people round you of misplacing it.

13. You went to see a movie with a group of people. Everyone has a different opinion. You:

A. Don't share your opinion.
B. Express your opinion but in a way that accommodates both sides.
C. Clearly express your opinion.
D. Try to convince others that your view is correct.

Add up your answers and find out your results on the next page...

Mostly 'A's: You are an introvert

You are quiet, reserved and thoughtful. You prefer to observe than participate. Big events can leave you feeling exhausted and drained – you recharge by having time on your own. Sometimes you can get overlooked, which is a shame, because you are an independent thinker, not swayed by trends or social pressure. Try not to hide in your shell – challenge yourself in small ways every day. Share your thoughts and feelings with others and try not to feel insecure about them.

Your opinions are valid and important!

Mostly 'B's: You are a public introvert, private extrovert

When you're with your inner circle, you are completely comfortable and confident, but when you're in wider group setting you can feel very shy and hold yourself back. You are sensitive and emotional, and you shine in your own quiet way. Sometimes you might take too much shelter in your comfort zone. Push yourself out to test your limits.

Mostly 'C's: You are a reluctant extrovert

You are outgoing and enthusiastic. You like being noticed, but there's a part of you that holds back and watches from outside. Beneath that confident exterior you can sometimes be filled with self-doubt and anxiety. Don't hide from your emotions by staying busy all the time. Stay with them so that they can provide a guide for your energy and ideas.

Mostly 'D's: You are an extrovert!

You are the life and soul of the party, the leader of the pack. At home and at school you feel confident sharing your thoughts and feelings and you don't worry too much about how people might respond. You recharge from being around other people and don't like spending time alone. Take some time to listen and to reflect on things. Be aware that other people might be less confident than you. Sharing the spotlight won't make you any less compelling!

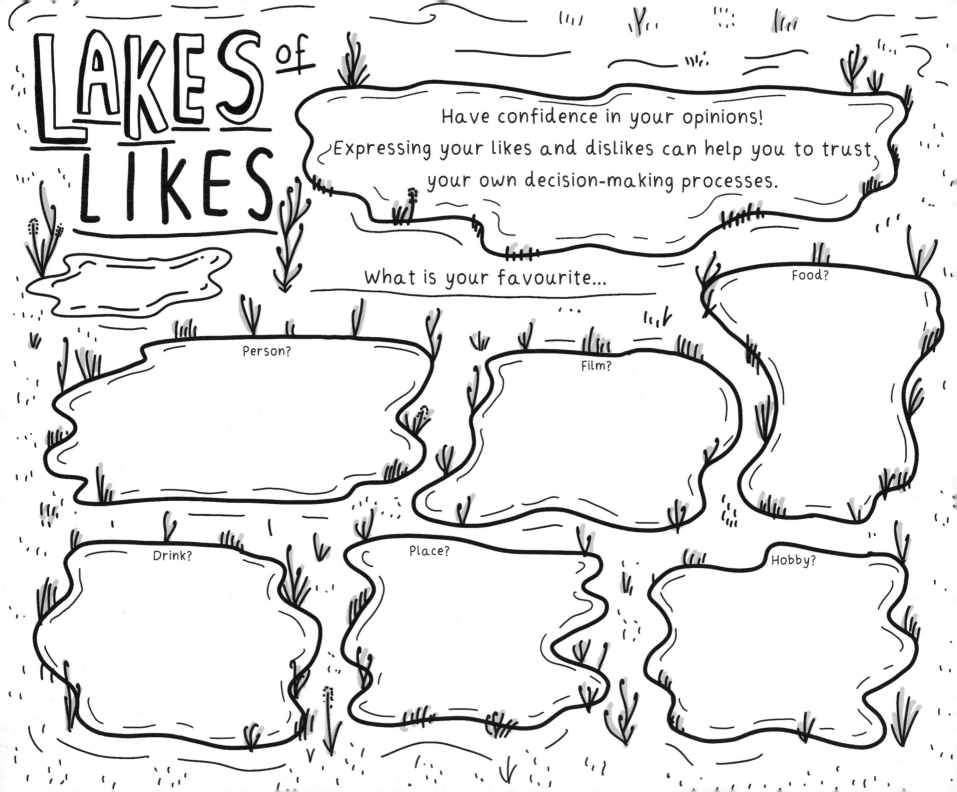

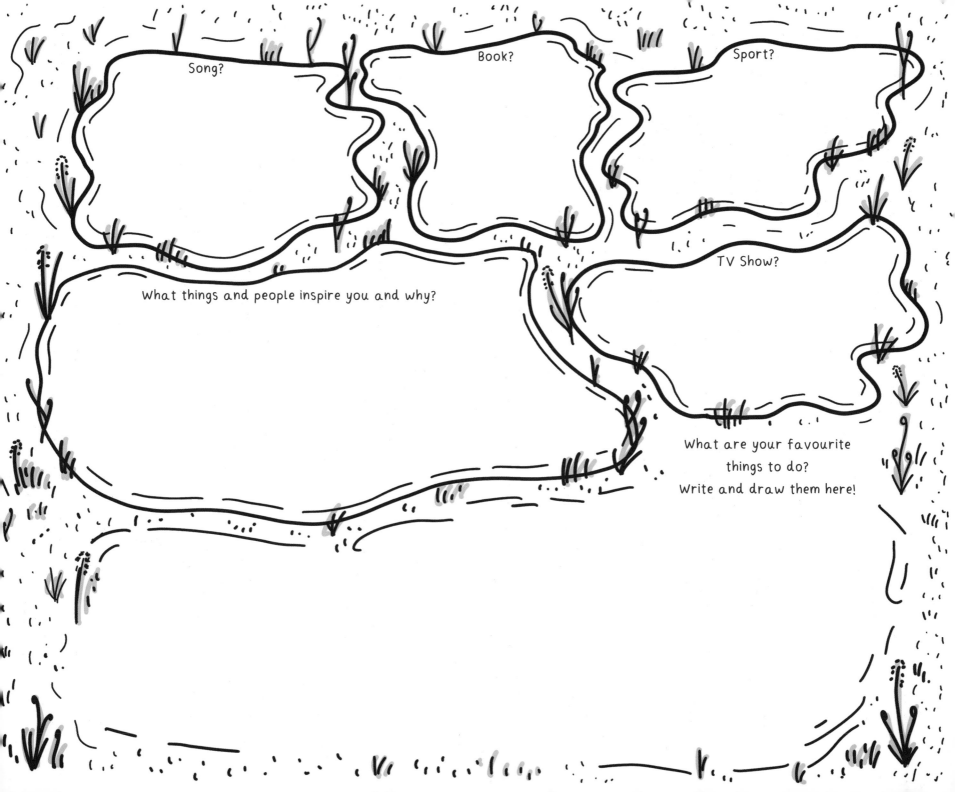

Song?

Book?

Sport?

TV Show?

What things and people inspire you and why?

What are your favourite
things to do?
Write and draw them here!

DESERT of DISLIKES

If you don't like something, ask yourself why. Is it something you genuinely don't connect to, or is it coming from a place of fear or discomfort that might be worth challenging?

What is your LEAST favourite....

Film?

Song?

Hobby?

Food?

Drink?

Place?

Book?

Sport?

TV Show?

Animal?

Chore?

Subject?

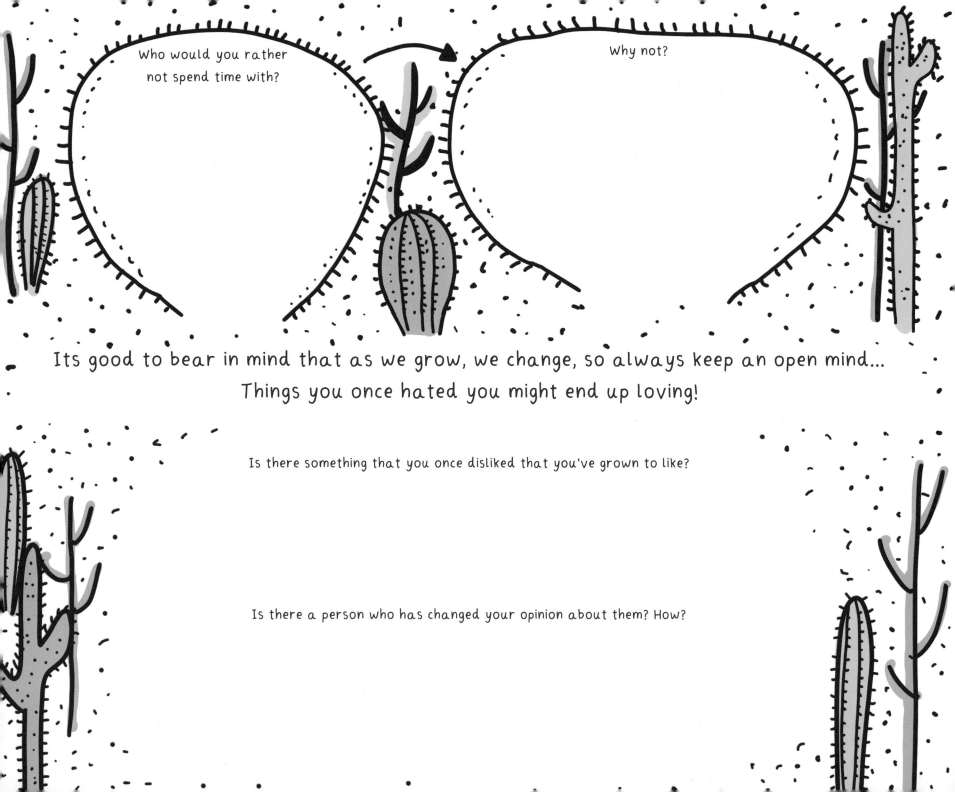

Who would you rather not spend time with?

Why not?

Its good to bear in mind that as we grow, we change, so always keep an open mind...
Things you once hated you might end up loving!

Is there something that you once disliked that you've grown to like?

Is there a person who has changed your opinion about them? How?

KINDNESS COVE ♡

Everyone carries their own complex landscape within, and we never know how someone else might be struggling, even if they seem outwardly confident. That's why kindness is so important. It costs nothing but means everything!

Has someone ever shown you kindness when you needed it most? Describe it here:

_____
_____
_____
_____
_____

What's an act of kindness that you have done for someone else? How did that person respond?

_____
_____
_____
_____
_____
_____

Be kind whenever possible. It is always possible.
– Dalai Lama

FRUITS of FRIENDSHIP ♥

Unlike family, we get to choose our friends. We pick them for lots of different reasons — each friendship nourishes us in a different way. Some friends are loyal and reliable and others are just fun to be around; some last a lifetime and others might just be here for a season...

What do you value in a friendship?

_____
_____
_____
_____

What makes you a good friend?

_____
_____
_____
_____

Organise these qualities in order of importance to you:

kind, reliable, creative, supportive, honest, loyal, patient, funny, spontaneous, inspiring, trustworthy, understanding, exciting

Most important: _____
_____
_____
_____
_____
_____
_____
_____
_____
_____
_____
Least important: _____

What qualities would you like to improve on to be the best friend you can be?

_____
_____
_____
_____
_____
_____

F.R.I.E.N.D.S.

Fight for you
Respect you
Include You
Encourage you
Need you
Deserve you
Stand by you

Think about the friendships in your life and put them into the friendship tree. Which ones are firmly rooted and which ones are blossoming fruits?

A friend is someone who helps you up when you're down, and if they can't, they lay down beside you and listen.
— Winnie the Pooh

lagoon of LONELINESS

When we are low on confidence, it can seem that we are unworthy of friendship and we can find ourselves feeling isolated and misunderstood. Research has found that one in five young people feel lonely 'most of the time' or 'always'.

Answer these yes or no questions to see how you are affected by loneliness:

Do you feel comfortable in yourself?
Yes   No

Do you feel happy around others?
Yes   No

Do you find it easy to make new friends?
Yes   No

Do you keep in touch regularly with your friends?
Yes   No

Do you have people in your life you feel close with?
Yes   No

Do you have much in common with the people around you?
Yes   No

Do you feel accepted and understood by others?
Yes   No

Mostly Yes - you are outgoing and content. Loneliness doesn't seem to be affecting you at the moment.

Mostly No - loneliness is something you experience. These are some things you can do to help manage those feelings.

Give yourself time to feel sadness

Let it wash over you so that calmer waters can follow.

Reach out

It can be harder than it sounds, but when we connect and share our feelings we can regain some control.

Get out of your head

Don't listen to the voice that says you're not worthy. We need to be a friend to ourselves and treat ourselves with the same kindness with which we treat the people we love.

Be generous

Helping others around you will make you appreciate the good things in your life and help you feel better about yourself.

Exercise

Sometimes loneliness is a state of mind. Moving our bodies releases hormones that relax our brains, helping us to see the world more clearly.

ISLANDS of ISOLATION

Being alone is not the same as being lonely. When we spend time on our own, we can allow our minds to wander without social distractions and pressures, giving us time to explore who we are and where our true interests lie. Time alone with your thoughts can build confidence and open up new creative pathways.

How do you feel about spending time on your own? Is it something you enjoy or does it stress you out?

If you could transport yourself to a desert island, would you go? For how long? Describe how it feels to be alone on your desert island.

What activities do you enjoy doing on your own?

What things would you take with you to the desert island?

Make a date with yourself – if you could spend an afternoon doing anything you like on your own, what would it be? Would you watch a movie on your own? Go to the park? Bake a cake?

Plan it here:

MEMORY MARSH

Today's moments are tomorrow's memories. Think about some of the most precious moments in your life and how those memories have shaped you as a person.

What is your earliest memory?

Write or draw it here:

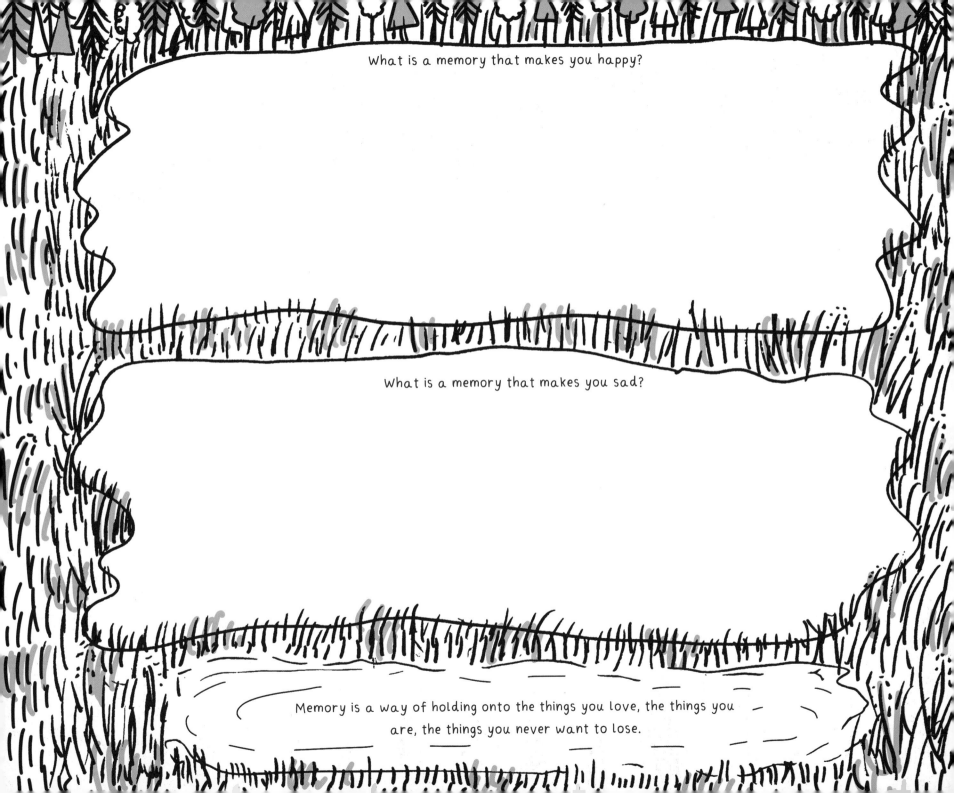

What is a memory that makes you happy?

What is a memory that makes you sad?

Memory is a way of holding onto the things you love, the things you
are, the things you never want to lose.

NIGHT FRIGHTS

Night time is when we should be switching our brains off,
but sometimes this is easier said than done!

What keeps you awake at night?

Write something that felt like a huge worry at night but in the
morning seemed much more manageable:

Some night time tips:

An hour before bed, write down all the things that might stress you out in the night. Write a plan of action for each one.

Avoid screens in the two hours before bed. Too much stimulation will get your brain whirring and also the blue light can disrupt your sleep hormones.

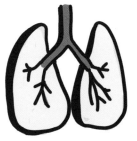

Write a gratitude list of good things about your day and all the things you are grateful for.

Build a routine. Half an hour before bed, do something relaxing like reading or listening to calming music. Do the same every night so that your brain knows it's time to start winding down.

Practice four-seven-eight breathing: inhale for for a count of four, hold for seven counts, and then blow out for eight counts. Do this five to seven times to slow your heart rate down.

Focus on your body: as you lie in bed, tense and relax all of your muscles one by one, starting at your toes and ending at your head to stay present and mindful.

PEAKS of PERFECTION

We live in an imperfect world, but some people can't help striving for perfection. Are you one of them? Take the quiz below to find out whether you're a perfectionist.

	Strongly Agree	Agree	Neutral	Disagree	Strongly Disgree
The only way I'm ever satisfied with my work is if it's done perfectly.	O	O	O	O	O
When I don't do well on a test I feel like a failure as a person.	O	O	O	O	O
I think that if I'm perfect, people will want to be my friends.	O	O	O	O	O
If I forget my homework, or don't complete my schoolwork, others will think I'm lazy.	O	O	O	O	O
I worry that if I don't get top marks, my parents will be disappointed in me.	O	O	O	O	O
On a group project I have to tell everyone what to do or they won't do it properly.	O	O	O	O	O
I am never proud of my achievements.	O	O	O	O	O

	Strongly Agree	Agree	Neutral	Disagree	Strongly Disagree
I feel like I need to please people all the time and I hate it when people don't like me.	O	O	O	O	O
I would rather not do something than do it badly.	O	O	O	O	O
I sometimes spend a very long time finishing a simple task because I want to get it exactly right.	O	O	O	O	O
I hate the thought of being average.	O	O	O	O	O
I don't like trying new things in front of other people.	O	O	O	O	O
I compare myself constantly to the people around me.	O	O	O	O	O
I can be impatient with my friends and family if I feel they're doing things wrong.	O	O	O	O	O
When I completed the other activities in this book, I did them to the best of my abilities with few or no mistakes.	O	O	O	O	O

Strongly agree = 5 points
Agree = 4 points
Neutral = 3 points
Disagree = 2 points
Strongly disagree = 1 point

Add up your points!

Total score :

If you scored 20 - 30 you are easy breezy!

You live in the moment — life is about the journey, not the end result! You're easy going and you never give yourself or others a hard time. Sometimes this might mean that you don't complete tasks to the best of your ability, or let yourself off the hook too easily. Try setting the bar just a fraction higher so that you can take pride in all the amazing things that you can do!

If you scored 30 - 50 you are a healthy realist!

You know that life can be messy and you don't give yourself a hard time about it. You make mistakes and you learn from them. You don't worry too much about what other people think. It's more important to stay true to yourself.

If you scored 50 - 60 you are a high achiever with some perfectionist qualities.

You set standards for yourself that are high, but achievable. You worry about failure and disapproval and give yourself a hard time when things don't go to plan, but you also enjoy the journey and know that you can't be perfect all of the time!

If you scored 60 - 75 you are a perfectionist!

You are an all-or-nothing type of person. If you don't meet your goals to the highest possible standard, you feel like a failure, but you're setting yourself an impossible task! Try to move through your perfectionism. Sometimes it's hard to compromise, but don't let perfect be the enemy of good!

TIME CAPSULE

Look back at yourself when you were younger. What words of advice
would you give younger you? Write them a letter!

Now think about your future self. What do you want to hold onto and never forget, even when life gets in the way? Fill this time capsule with objects that capture your life right now at this moment in time. Draw the objects and write what they are. You don't need to say why they're significant – future you will have to work that out for themselves!

TIME CAPSULE

STARS of DREAMS

You've made it to the end of Map of You, but the real journey of self-discovery will last your whole life. You'll never stop growing and evolving and learning about yourself...

Draw yourself as a shining star in the night sky:

Now all that's left to do is set off into the universe! Remember, you can achieve ANYTHING you put your mind to!

Take some time to reflect on your journey and also to think about where you want to go next.

Write down some things you have learned about yourself:

_____
_____
_____
_____
_____
_____
_____

Write down what you are going to do next:

_____
_____
_____
_____
_____
_____

Write down the things that make you shine:

_____
_____
_____
_____
_____
_____
_____

Write down your aspirations for the future:

_____
_____
_____
_____
_____
_____

It is not in the stars to hold our destiny but in ourselves.

– William Shakespeare

About the Author

Sophie Williams is an illustration graduate from Winchester School of Art. Her work takes inspiration from illustrators such as Nick Sharratt and Gemma Correll, as well as the beautiful surroundings of her home in Cornwall. Her own struggles with anxiety led her to create *Map of You* for her graduate project.

(That's me!)

Acknowledgements

I would like to say thank you to all the rocks in my life - my incredible friends and family. I'm so lucky to have so much love and support in my life. These are the people that got me through my struggles to where I am now, writing and illustrating my own book! Massive thanks to Ziggy for guiding me through the book-writing process and helping turn my dream into reality. I would also like to say a special thanks to the biggest rock in my life — to Rob — you are the centre of my world.

And lastly, this book is dedicated to my animal guides - Coco, Buddy and Chip. The most special angels I've had the pleasure to know.

Map of You

Text and illustration © Sophie Williams

British Library Cataloguing-in-Publication Data.

A CIP record for this book is available from the British Library

ISBN: 978-1-80066-015-1

First published in the UK, 2021, in the USA, 2022

Cicada Books Ltd

48 Burghley Road

London, NW5 1UE

www.cicadabooks.co.uk

Printed in Poland